SMART BRAIN RIGHT BRAIN

# An Introduction to Mobile Phone Technology

Om KIDZ
An imprint of Om Books International

**Om Books International**

Reprinted in 2023

**Corporate & Editorial Office**
A-12, Sector 64, Noida 201 301
Uttar Pradesh, India
Phone: +91 120 477 4100
Email: editorial@ombooks.com
Website: www.ombooksinternational.com

**Sales Office**
107, Ansari Road, Darya Ganj
New Delhi 110 002, India
Phone: +91 11 4000 9000
Email: sales@ombooks.com



Author: Shweta Sinha
Editor: Kirti Pathak
Art & Design: Anshuman Pandey, Gaurav Bhandari, Harish Arya

ISBN: 978-93-52768-41-7

Printed in India

10 9 8 7 6 5 4 3 2

# CONTENTS

# 1. A Thing Called Telephone

A telephone is a communication tool. People use it to talk to others who are far away. The telephone was invented by a scientist named Alexander Graham Bell in 1876. Since then people throughout the world have not stopped calling each other.

The early telephones were directly connected with wires. So, you couldn't call your friends if their phones weren't wired to yours.

Today's mobile phones are way different from those early telephones.

**DID YOU KNOW?**

A telephone exchange allows a telephone to call another telephone, without the two being directly wired.

## Activity: Make your own wired telephone

You need: Two paper cups, a long piece of string.

1. Make holes in the bottom of both cups.

2. Tie the ends of the string through each hole, such that the backs of the cups face each other.

3. Have a friend take one cup, while you take the other. Stand far apart and stretch the string. Ensure it does not touch anything.

4. Speak into your cup. Can your friend hear what you said?

You can now talk on your 'wired telephone'.

# 2. From Wired to Wireless

The original telephone was an electric device. It needed wires to transmit sound. Telephones connected with wires are called fixed or **landline telephones**.

Landline phones are still in use today, but their technology has changed. They are now electronic and send digital signals.

**DID YOU KNOW?** The first words spoken on a telephone were, "Mr. Watson- come here, I want to see you!" by Alexander G. Bell to his assistant on 10 March 1876.

# Wireless Telephones

Wireless or cordless telephones can send sound over radio signals. Radio is a way to send information over a long distance.

Televisions, Wi-Fi connections, FM radio - all use radio signals.

A mobile or a cellphone is a type of wireless telephone. It is a small, portable radio telephone.

**POCKET FACT**

**Like walkie-talkies, mobile phones run on battery power.**

# 3. The Story of Mobile Phones

Radio was first used to send telegraph messages without wires. It was a fast way to communicate where mail would take days to reach. Telegraph was especially useful in ships sailing on the sea. They used telegraph to communicate with the shore and other ships.

Soon, we had walkie-talkies that let people talk using radio signals. This finally led to the invention of mobile phones

**DID YOU KNOW?**

When radio signals are sent out to many people at the same time, it is called a 'broadcast'.

At first, mobile phones were really large and heavy. They were mostly built into cars. These were actually meant for people, like truck drivers, to talk to emergency services. These early mobile phones also cost a lot.

Technology improved and mobile phones became smaller and lighter. However, mobile phones did not become popular until the late 1980s.

**POCKET FACT**

In 1973, the first mobile call was made using a device that weighed 1.1 kg.

# Mobile phones over the years

Ask your parents about mobile phones from when they were kids. Were the phones like the ones we have today? If your parents don't remember, you can show them here.

**1982** - The year saw the first true mobile phone for the public. This Nokia phone weighed more than a newborn baby!

**1983** - This phone model weighed only 1 kg, but a fully charged battery worked for only 30 minutes.

**1992** - After ten long years, Nokia launched its 1011 model. It weighed only 500 gm and could be used anywhere in the world. More people began using mobile phones.

**1997** - Siemens rocked the world with a new colour screen mobile phone.

**2000** - Mobile phones now had digital cameras. Development in mobile technology picked up pace in the new century.

**2003** - Mobile phones with advanced features such as cameras and internet access, were becoming popular. The 'Quark' by Blackberry also offered instant messaging service. This model changed the way we communicated. People moved from using emails to messaging.

**2007**- Apple launched the i-Phone. This started the era of smartphones. Today, we use phones not just to call and send texts, but to do almost everything, like paying bills and to keeping track of our fitness.

**DID YOU KNOW?**

The first mobile phones were sold for a whopping 4000 US dollars!

# Types of Mobile Phones

All mobile phones have a screen for display and a keypad to type. They run on a battery that needs to be recharged from time to time.

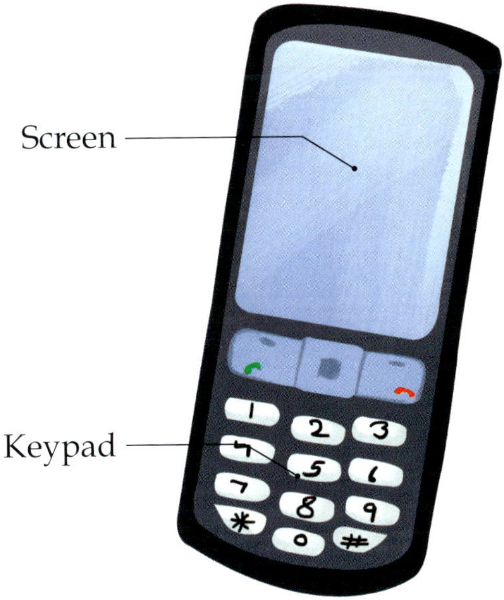


Mobile phones come in many different shapes and sizes.

- Bar phones that are shaped like candy bars.
- Flip phones have a section that folds and covers the keypad and screen.
- Slider phones that can slide out the keypad.
- Slate phones that have almost no keys.

**POCKET FACT**

**Most smartphones are slates. The keypad appears on the screen only when needed.**

# 4. Mobile Phone and its Friends

A mobile phone cannot work alone. It needs mobile network services. Unlike walkie-talkie sets that connect directly, mobile phones connect through a service provider.

A **service provider** is a company that lets you call another phone. Service providers create a network of cell towers. Mobile phones connect to these towers to send and receive signals.

In the beginning, only one base tower connected phones in a large area. If you moved out of the area during a call, your call got disconnected. Also, only a few phones could be connected to a base tower.

In 1970, a new system allowed mobile phones to hop from one tower to another. This system was called the "call handoff". It enabled mobiles to stay connected even while moving from one area to another.

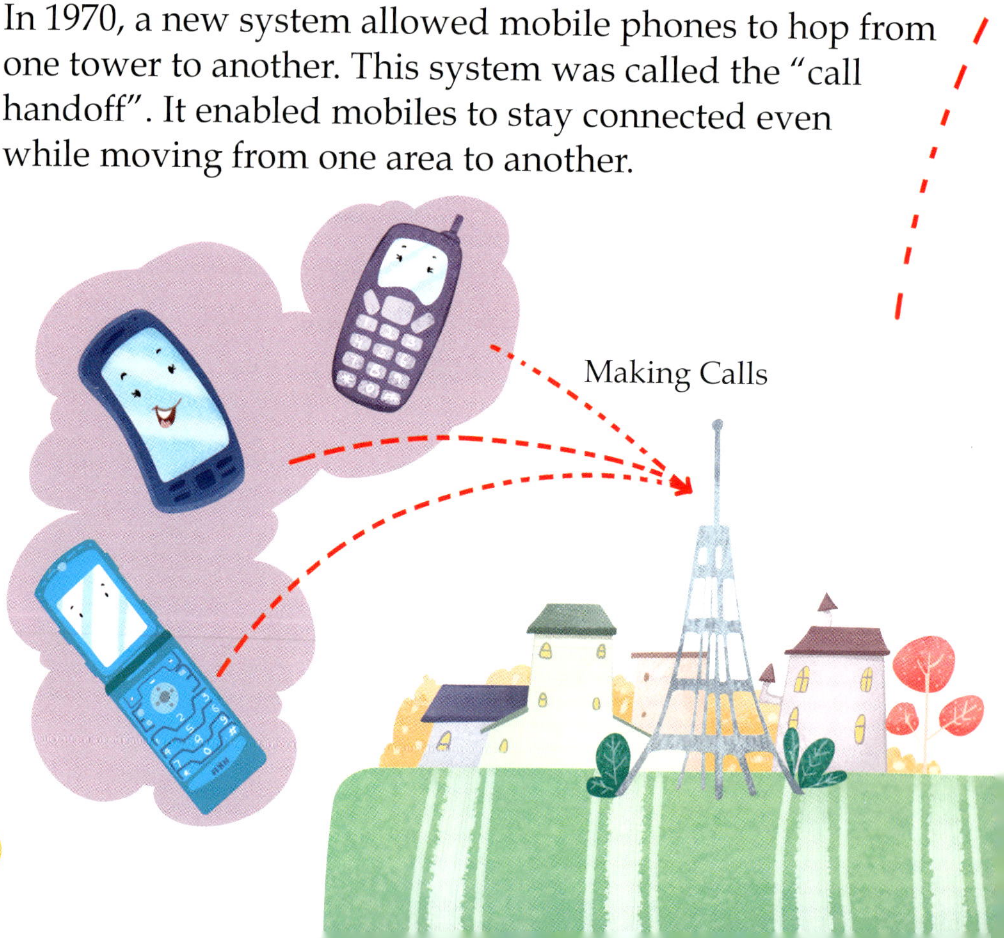

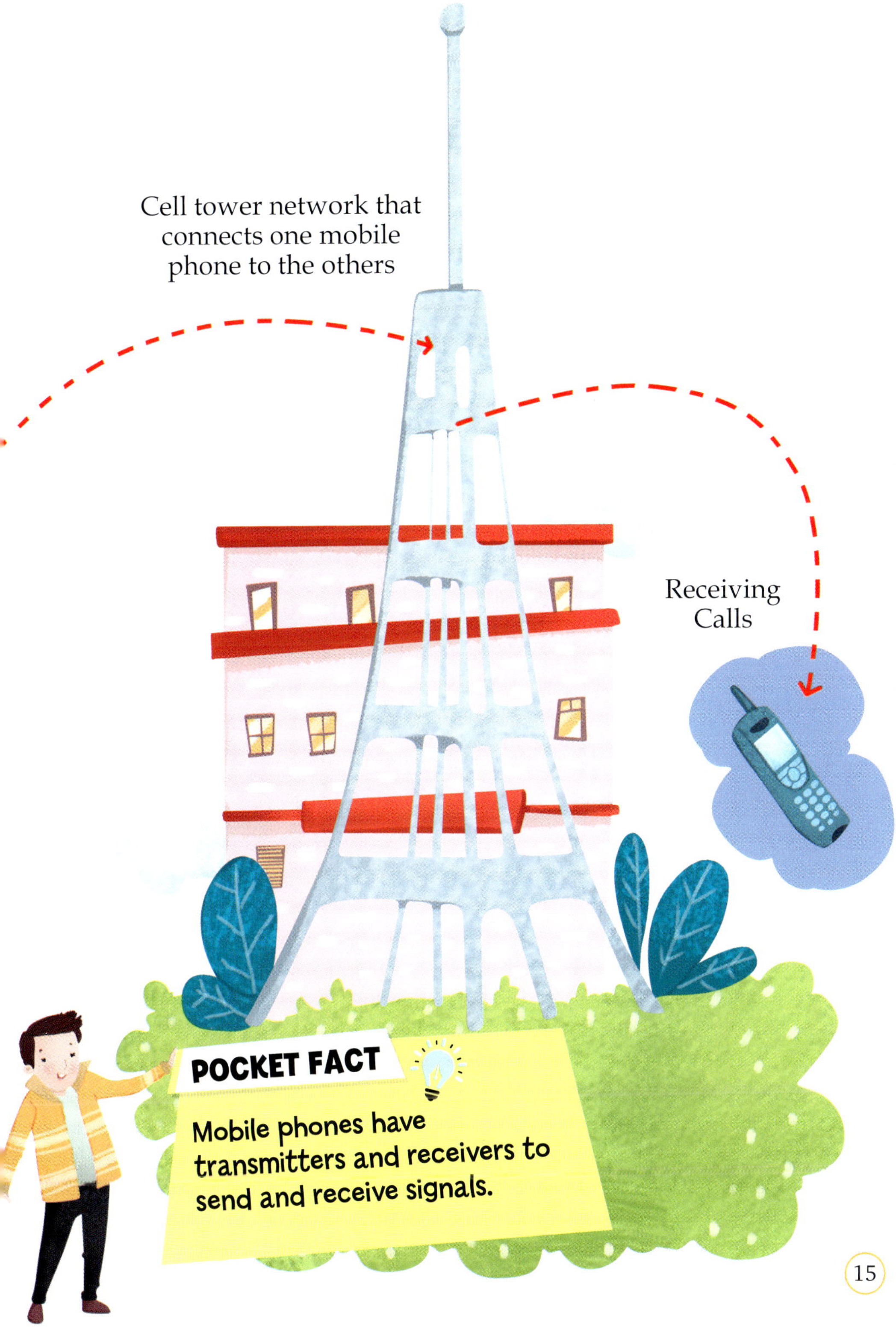


**POCKET FACT**

Mobile phones have transmitters and receivers to send and receive signals.

# Mobile Networks

Mobile networks are made of "cells". A cell is an area of land that is typically shaped like a hexagon. Each cell has one transceiver cell tower. These "cells" connect to one another. A mobile network is a complex web of these connected tower zones.

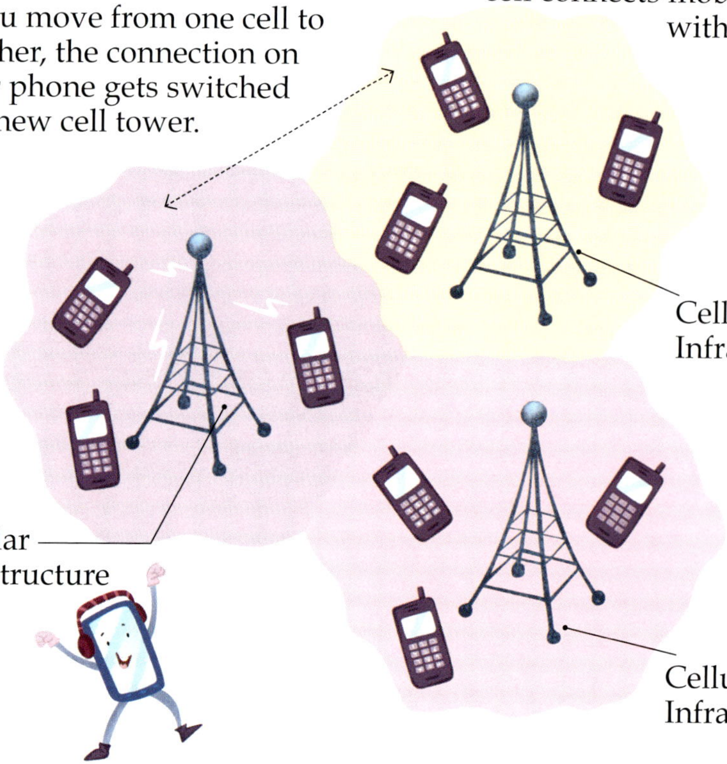


**DID YOU KNOW?** Mobile networks are also called cellular networks as they are made up of "cells".

# 5. How Do Mobile Phones Work?

A mobile phone is not a mysterious device, it is simply a two-way radio. When you talk with your friend, your mobile converts your voice into electric signals. The signals are then transmitted to the nearest cell tower as radio waves. The radio waves get passed from one cell tower to the next. Finally, it reaches your friend's mobile. Your friend's mobile converts the radio waves back to electric signals and then to voice.

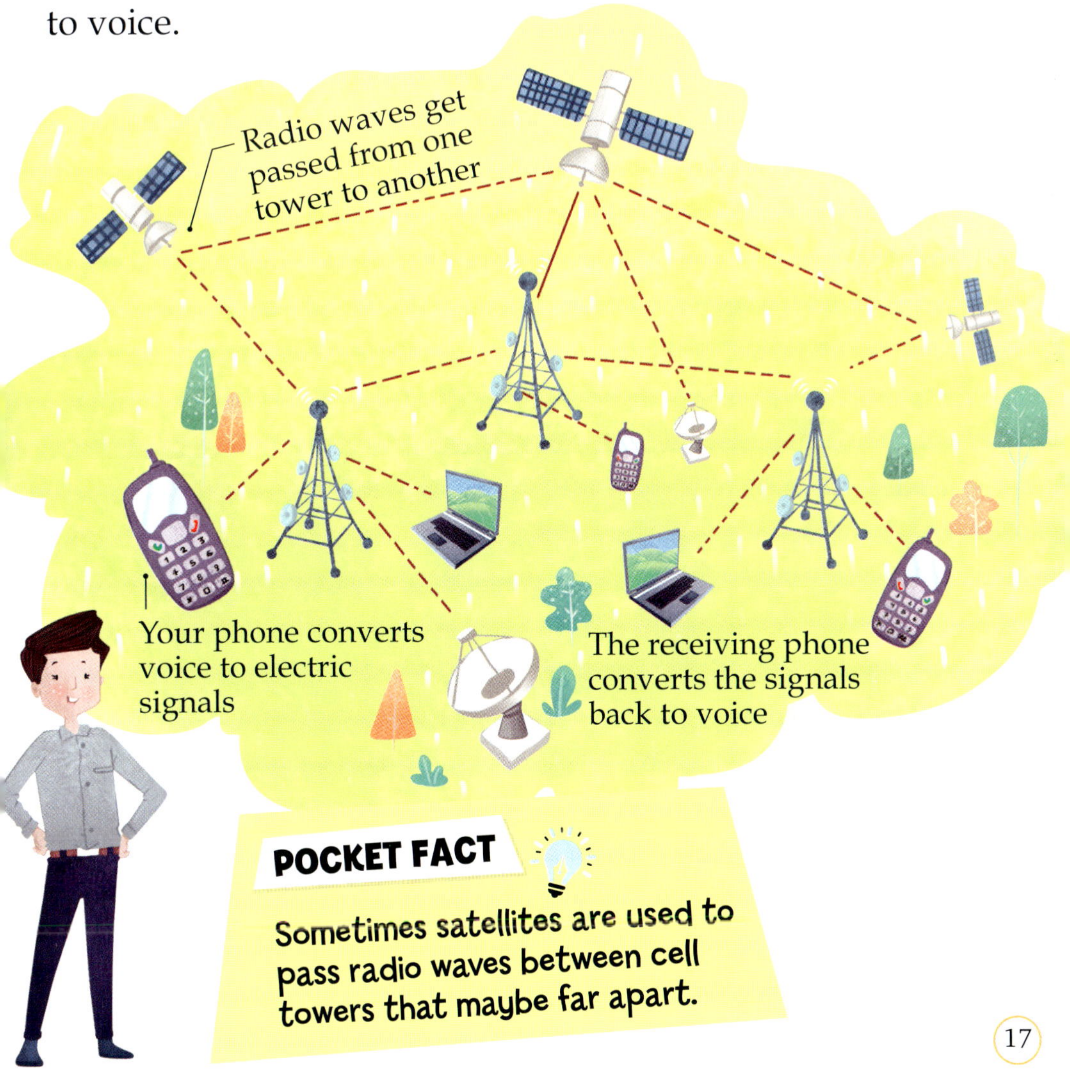


**POCKET FACT**

Sometimes satellites are used to pass radio waves between cell towers that maybe far apart.

# Why do we need phone numbers?

Every telephone in the world has a number. It is like a unique 'address' for the phone. It helps locate the phone in the world.

Every country has a country code. To call a phone in another country, you need to add the country code before the phone number.

We can save other people's phone numbers on our mobile phones. Before mobile phones, people wrote down numbers in a phone diary. They also used a telephone directory. A telephone directory was simply a book of phone numbers.

**POCKET FACT**

In the early days, phones had no numbers. People called a telephone operator and asked to be connected to a particular line.

# Funny Faces

Do you know what these funny faces are? They are called **emojis**. People send emojis in instant messages to show their feelings. Emojis were invented in 1999 in Japan. Before emojis, people used text-based emoticons.

Guess what feelings these emoticons and emojis represent:

| Emoticon | Emoji | Feeling |
| --- | --- | --- |
| :-) |  | |
| :-( |  | |
| :-D |  | |
| >:( |  | |

**DID YOU KNOW?**

**The first text message was sent on 3 December 1992. It read "Merry Christmas".**

# 3G, 4G and 5G Networks

Just like the mobile phones, their networks too have evolved over the years.

Major improvements were marked as a 'Generation' (G).

- **Early Generations:**

The early phones with limited networks are often called 'Zero Generation' phones.

The next two generations, 1G and 2G, improved the network coverage. Second Generation (2G) made it possible to use a mobile phone from anywhere in the world . 2G also introduced texting or SMS.

- **Third Generation (3G):**

3G services increased the speed of the mobile signals. It gave access to data connections. When you use internet on your mobile, you are using the mobile's data connection.

- **Fourth Generation (4G):**

4G further increased the speed of data connections. It was up to 10 times faster than 3G. High speed allowed us to watch videos and listen to music on our mobile phones.

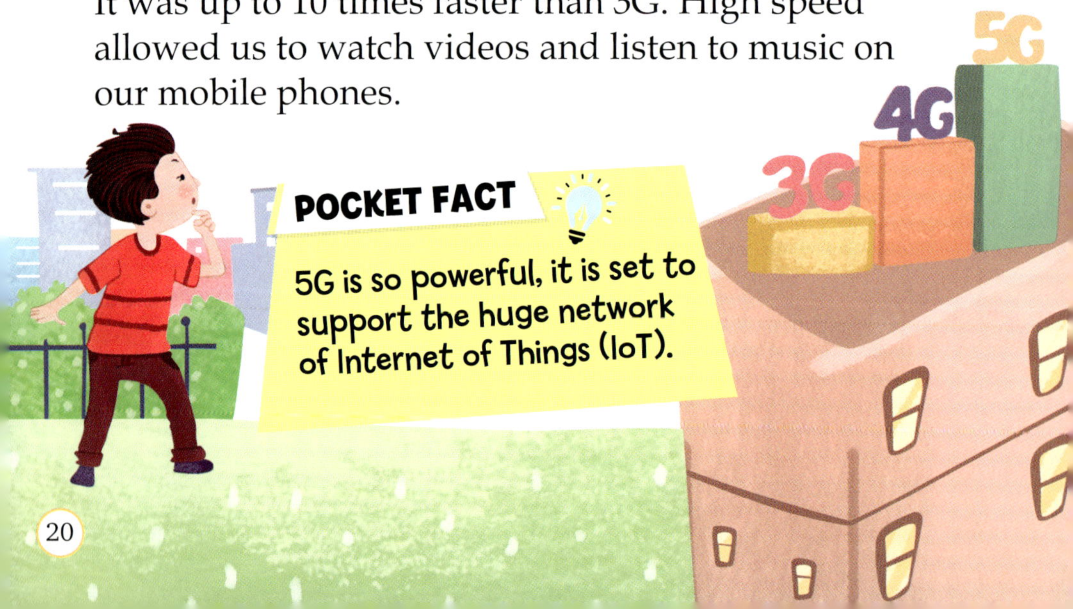


**POCKET FACT**

5G is so powerful, it is set to support the huge network of Internet of Things (IoT).

# What comes next?

3G introduced mobile data and 4G gave us high-speed internet access. The latest 5G technology promises to connect more devices at ultrafast speeds. It will be so fast, it may even replace the wired internet connection at your home.

**DID YOU KNOW?**

Nepal's cellular service company, Ncell, provides 3G services on top of Mount Everest.

# 6. The Smartphone Era

In 2007, Apple's i-Phone ushered in the smartphone era. After Apple, other companies introduced their own smartphones in the market. But, what is a smartphone, anyway?

A smartphone is a mobile phone that does much more than the other phones. It works like a computer. Yet, it is small enough to fit in your hand. Most new phones in the 21st century are smartphones.

**DID YOU KNOW?**

In 1993, IBM launched a mobile phone with a touchscreen just like a smartphone.

Smartphones have completely changed the way people work and communicate. People have moved from using personal computers to smartphones now.

- Smartphones are fast, very fast.
- They make it easier to browse the World Wide Web.
- Smartphones have replaced paper maps.
- We can do shopping from our phones.
- We can watch movies and listen to music anywhere.
- They also help us take pictures and make videos.
- And, we can also call and send messages.

**POCKET FACT**

Most smartphones run on 3 G or 4G networks.

# Apps and app stores

Everything you see on a mobile phone is an app. An app is a computer program that makes your phone useful. The game, the maps and even the camera are all types of apps.

You can go to an app store or play store to install an app. An app store or play store is like a shop for apps.

App Store

Play Store

Some apps are free to use, but there are apps you need to pay for. Some apps can even harm your mobile. Do not download any app without asking your parents first.

**DID YOU KNOW?**

Programmers write apps using computer languages, like Java. You too can learn to write apps.

# 7. Mobile Phones: The Good and the Bad

Mobile phones are a great tool, but remember they can also be harmful.

Mobile phones can be expensive. Using them too much raises your phone bills.

So, it is important to know how to use them properly.

**Be a responsible mobile user:**

- Don't use anyone else's phone without asking.
- Take a parent's permission before using a mobile phone.
- Be careful of what you text someone. Be polite.
- Only text people whom you know in real life.
- Don't pass other's phone numbers without asking.
- Do not talk loudly over your phone in a public place.

**POCKET FACT**

Using all capital letters in a text message is like SHOUTING at someone.

# When it's NOT OK to use your phone

- Some places, like aeroplanes and hospitals, restrict mobile phones as phone signals affect their equipments. Switch off your phone at such places.
- It is rude to use a phone in movie theatres or libraries. The sound disturbs others.
- Schools usually do not allow students to carry mobile phones.
- Use your phone only when necessary. When you are with friends and family, it is more important to talk to them and to enjoy with them.

**DID YOU KNOW?**

Just like the good manners you follow every day, good manners when using a phone are important too.

# Staying Safe

What would you do if:

- You receive a message saying, "You are a loser".
- A friend sends you a gross picture.
- Someone calls you up to say hurtful things.

Tell a grownup right away. Remember, such kind of mean behaviour is called **cyber-bullying**. And it is against the law in many places.

## Safety Tip

Save ICE Numbers on your phone: ICE stands for 'In Case of Emergency'. These could be numbers of your parents or caregivers. It helps others contact them if you need help.

**POCKET FACT**

Never give out personal details, like your full name, birth date, address or school, to a caller you don't know.

## Find the correct sequence

Number these steps according to the correct sequence when you call a friend's mobile. The first one is done for you:

| | |
|---|---|
| | (a) Your friend's mobile receives the radio waves. |
| 1 | (b) Your mobile converts your voice into electric signals. |
| | (c) The radio waves get passed from one cell tower to the next. |
| | (d) The signals are transmitted to the nearest cell tower via radio waves. |
| | (e) Finally, it reaches your friend's mobile. |
| | (f) The mobile converts the radio waves back to electric signals and then to voice. |

## True or False

State whether the following statements are true or false:

1. 3G, 4G, 5G are names of mobile network generations. (True/False)
2. Smartphones are smart because they wear nice clothes. (True/False)
3. Wireless telegraphs were used by ships on sea. (True/False)
4. Mobile signals are sometimes sent through satellites. (True/False)
5. Cyber-bullying is harmless and is allowed. (True/False)
6. You should always send text messages in all capitals. (True/False)

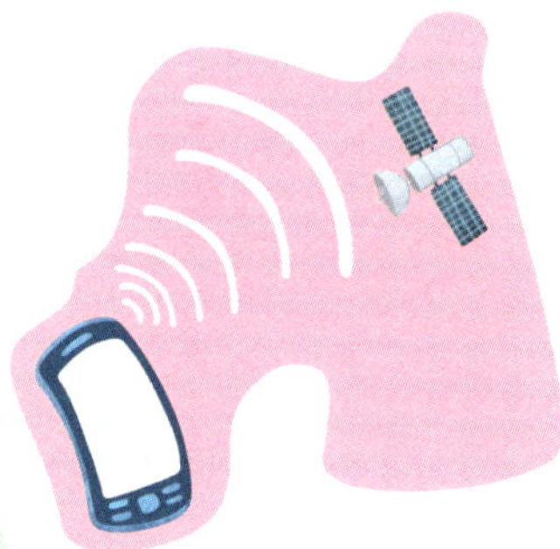

**Choose the correct answer:**

1. Who invented the telephone?

   (a) Albert Einstein

   (b) Alexander Graham Bell

   (c) Thomas Edison

2. What is a telephone that is connected with wires called?

   (a) Landline

   (b) Wireless

   (c) Cordless

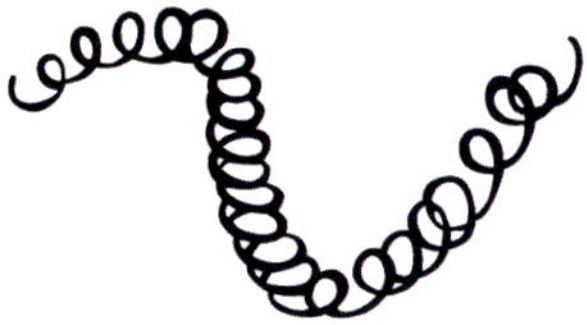

3. A mobile phone is a two-way ________

   (a) Television

   (b) Computer

   (c) Radio

4. What type is a smartphone?

   (a) Bar

   (b) Slate

   (c) Flip

5. A mobile network is made of areas of land shaped like a

   (a) Hexagon

   (b) Square

   (c) Circle

6. Funny faces that people send in text messages are called

   (a) Clowns

   (b) Images

   (c) Emojis

## Smart users for Smartphones

Tick the mobile phone usage that are correct and cross out the ones that aren't.

1. Use your mobile phone to click and send lots of videos to your friends.
2. Switch off your phone inside a movie theatre.
3. Save ICE numbers on your phone.
4. Talk loudly on a phone in public places.
5. Delete hurtful message you may have received and don't tell anyone.
6. Keep the phone away when you have dinner with your family.

## GLOSSARY

| | |
|---|---|
| Century | a hundred years |
| Communicate | to share information, news and ideas |
| Convert | to change from one form to another |
| Electric | something that runs on electricity |
| Electronic | a device containing components such as microchips |
| Emergency | a serious, unexpected, and often dangerous situation |
| Internet of Things | a network of everyday things that use the internet to communicate |
| Launch | introduce a new product to the public |
| Navigation | to find out a route to a destination and follow it |
| Radio wave | an electromagnetic wave used by television, radio, mobile phones etc. to transmit data over long distances |
| Receiver | an electronic device which picks up signals |
| Satellite | a natural or man-made object that orbits a planet |
| Technology | the use of science in solving problems |
| Telegraph | a device to transmit written messages over long distances |
| Telephone operator | people who helped customers place telephone calls |
| Transceiver | an electronic device that both sends and receives signals |
| Transmit | broadcast over the airwaves, as in radio or television |
| Transmitter | an electronic device which sends signals |

## ANSWERS

Page 28. 1. (b) 2. (d) 3. (c) 4. (e) 5. (a) 6. (f)

Page 29. 1. True 2. False 3. True 4. True 5. False 6. False

Page 30. 1. (b) 2.(a) 3.(c) 4. (b) 5.(a) 6.(c)

Page 31.
1. Wrong (×)- Sending too many videos will disturb others and raise your mobile bill.
2. Correct (√) - It is impolite to use a phone in a movie theatre.
3. Correct (√)- Saving ICE numbers help emergency services to contact your parents.
4. Wrong (×)- Talking loudly disturbs others.
5. Wrong (×)-This is cyber-bullying. Save the message and show it to an adult.
6. Correct (√)-Family and friends are more important than your mobile.